BLAZERS

The U.S. Armed Forces

The Blue Angels

by Carrie A. Braulick

Reading Consultant:
Barbara J. Fox
Reading Specialist
North Carolina State University

Capstone
press

Mankato, Minnesota

Blazers is published by Capstone Press,
151 Good Counsel Drive, P.O. Box 669, Mankato, Minnesota 56002.
www.capstonepress.com

Library of Congress Cataloging-in-Publication Data
Braulick, Carrie A., 1975–
    The Blue Angels / by Carrie A. Braulick.
      p. cm.—(Blazers—the U.S. Armed Forces)
    Includes bibliographical references and index.
    ISBN 0-7368-3793-0 (hardcover)
    1. United States. Naval Flight Demonstration Squadron—Juvenile literature.
I. Title. II. Series.
VG94.6.N38B73 2005
797.5'4—dc22   2004010535

Summary: Describes the U.S. Navy's Blue Angels, including their planes, the formations and maneuvers of their air shows, and team member duties.

Credits
Juliette Peters, set designer; Enoch Peterson and Steve Christensen, book designers;
    Jo Miller, photo researcher; Scott Thoms, photo editor

Photo Credits
AP/Wide World Photos/National Museum of Naval Aviation, 11
David O. Bailey, 25
DVIC/Kenn Mann, USAF CIV, 13; LCPL Ismael Marquez, USMC, 12
Getty Images Inc./Justin Sullivan, 8, 22–23
Navy Photo, cover (both), 26; PH1 Casey Akins, 6; PH1 Darryl Herring, 5; PH3
    Leah Wilson, 17
Photo by Ted Carlson/Fotodynamics, 7, 14, 18, 19 (both), 20, 21, 28–29

Capstone Press thanks Lieutenant Mike Blankenship, U.S. Navy Blue Angels, for his assistance in preparing this book.

1 2 3 4 5 6 10 09 08 07 06 05

Table of Contents

The Blue Angels in Action

The Blue Angel planes speed down the runway. They soar into the sky. The air show begins.

Four planes flip upside down. They
do a diamond dirty loop. Next, the
planes fly close to each other in a
fan formation.

Diamond dirty loop

Horizontal rolls

BLAZER FACT

The Blue Angels' name came from a business featured in the *New Yorker* magazine.

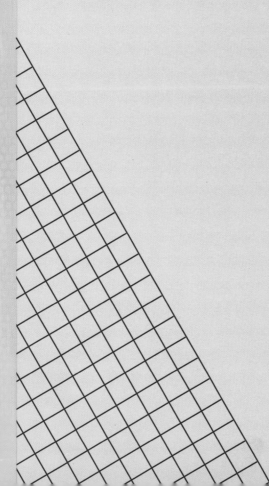

Two planes fly next to each
other. They roll sideways in a
circle. Later, the planes land
and the show ends.

Blue Angel Planes

Navy pilot Roy Voris formed the Blue Angels in 1946. The Blue Angels perform daring stunts with planes.

First Blue Angels team

Roy Voris

★★★★★★★★★★

11

The Blue Angels fly F/A-18 Hornets. These fighter jets are smaller and faster than many other planes.

A large C-130 Hercules
plane carries supplies
to Blue Angel air shows. The
Blue Angels call it Fat Albert.

BLAZER FACT

Fully loaded, Fat Albert
weighs more than
10 African elephants.

Formations and Maneuvers

Formations are part of each air show. The main formation is the delta.

Delta

★ ★ ★ ★ ★ ★

17

Other formations are the line abreast, echelon, and diamond. The planes almost touch each other in some formations.

Echelon

Diamond

BLAZER FACT

In the 1930s, the Gulfhawk II stunt plane was built to fly upside down for up to 30 minutes.

The Blue Angels are famous for their bold maneuvers. Two planes fly upside down in the double farvel. Six planes do rolls in the fleur-de-lis.

Fleur-de-lis

Delta Positions

Flight leader

Right wing

Opposing solo

Left wing

Lead solo

Slot

Blue Angel Jobs

Blue Angel pilots have many years of flying experience. They spend two years with the team.

★ ★ ★ ★ ★ ★ ★ ★ ★ ★ ★ ★ ★

Some Blue Angel members fix planes or plan shows. All members work together to make shows successful.

BLAZER FACT

During training season, Blue Angel pilots practice two times a day and six days a week.

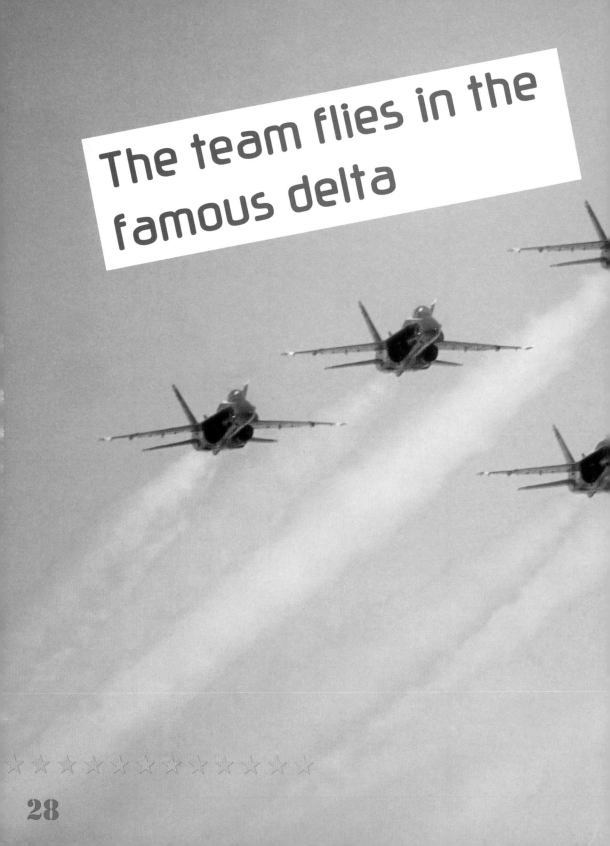

The team flies in the famous delta

Glossary

delta (DEL-tuh)—the main formation of the Blue Angels

diamond (DYE-muhnd)—a formation in which four Blue Angel planes form a diamond shape

echelon (e-SHUH-lawn)—a formation in which four Blue Angel planes line up diagonally

formation (for-MAY-shuhn)—a group of airplanes flying together in a pattern

maneuver (muh-NOO-ver)—a planned and controlled movement

roll (ROHL)—to turn sideways in a complete circle

runway (RUHN-way)—a strip of level land that aircraft use for taking off and landing

Read More

Bartlett, Richard. *United States Navy.* U.S. Armed Forces. Chicago: Heinemann, 2004.

Bledsoe, Glen, and Karen Bledsoe. *The Blue Angels: The U.S. Navy Flight Demonstration Squadron.* Serving Your Country. Mankato, Minn.: Capstone Press, 2001.

Cooper, Jason. *U.S. Navy.* Fighting Forces. Vero Beach, Fla.: Rourke, 2004.

Internet Sites

FactHound offers a safe, fun way to find Internet sites related to this book. All of the sites on FactHound have been researched by our staff.

Here's how:

1. Visit *www.facthound.com*
2. Type in this special code **0736837930** for age-appropriate sites. Or enter a search word related to this book for a more general search.
3. Click on the **Fetch It** button.

FactHound will fetch the best sites for you!

Index